LONESPEECH

nightboat books

new york

ann jäderlund

LONESPEECH

translated by johannes göransson

probably a star still has light

paul celan

but not tonight let us find the words

ingeborg bachmann

ISBN: 978-1-64362-236-1

Cover design and interior typesetting by Kit Schluter
Typeset in Neue Kabel and Futura PT

Cataloging-in-publication data is available
from the Library of Congress

Nightboat Books
New York
www.nightboat.org

LONESPEECH

The sun dies
open the window
and do fly
if you want to
fly

The voice burns
I can see the word
it goes through the eye
from hearing
it is poisonous
with clear velocity
speak you too

Up on the mountain
there are trees and rivers
and behind the mountain
other mountains
what the river wants
no one knows
it runs
it runs
lord

The sun goes in the aorta
the word for darkness
hides a dark sound
then what's at stake

Awe
it is burst
even there
raw and
clearabout
clearabout
it is burst

Can we find the words
today we say today
it burns today
the river runs
can we guess
one by one
it burns today

Along the river

there are

stones

and mountains that

run

wolf beans

lupines

every seed in

the sack.

crowded against

the

others

tick

talk

you were

able to

do that

Stand so that the wind
blows on you
from the kitchen
the kitchen is a chamber
that goes on the head
in the air you are
made of air
I have
been
stabbed to
the brains

The sun lets its light out
over the window
which does not exist
its light
which does not exist
it was another light
and now it is also
something else

All have needs
needs in their eyes
fists
contorted river mountain
at home the words are
at home

Forest black
all clang
forest black
black
forehead
foreclang
I want to hear

Multireversable
and lost
it comes back
again
lard
alongside
alone
seeps through
but what
when the arnica
blooms yellow
the yellow
spot
becomes
visible
it is said

How curious
everything without
almost everyone
everything
everything
unshafted
without

We scoop the sounds
scoop and moan
it cannot be
taken away
with words
but it
goes away
with the words

Nor did
they
see
each other
or after
them
can they still
speak do they
speak with

The mountain
the forest
someone did it
someone fell
kept away
someone appeared
to enjoy someone
enjoyed
the ears are exposed
to many
sounds I
am alone

You yourself cut
up the eye
or pricked it
with a
thin needle
I understand that
not even
a second
a single
second

Before the limit is reached

comes a moment

that quickly passes

or even had time

to exist

the smoke goes into the eye

the eye into the smoke

also they have

only that grave

Right hand
not by my hand
right eye
which waits and stings
maybe was cut out of
the left preceding
scoop and fray
gnaws

Clang earth
root worry
about will
will
clang worry
earth root

The eye
the neck
is it the window
the sun
the sun
only words

It burns
today can
you answer
I cannot
hear
speak

Inversion

of black

Black Forest

as the forest black

gets colors

all colors

that still do not exist

and can be measured

Can we listen
it hides
bends itself
today
today we say
today but
where
where is
it

Surely a star has
no light
if it has
light
more than both matter

Ice home
field
that's what
it becomes
but not
if it
becomes

Each and every one

with one

with its one

enclosed one

about their one

and one

clang

noneabout

summer

Sounds about sounds meld
one can hear them
not at the ears
near near
then one hears another
sound word

No one has names

no one

perianth's fingers

all are poisonous

Little flower
you burst

Blow trees
beneath the music
in the forest blow
trees
I swallow lights
I swallow
it
which is
in front of me
pull out
the ground

Where are you
where will
you be
this summer
I hear
the hands
the river

Everything is
equally strange

Speak say
hear
listen
some
someone
has time

Clang

noneabout

summer

come clang

come be

the same

noneabout

clang

the same

come come

be

In the forest
air and rooted
tree trunks
gnaw against
each other
fate
everything is chance
and fate
in life
blessed are you
and mercy is what
you bring
that moment
earth joy
lack loneliness
air
joy

None have names

everyone knows it

but hear

only names

names and names

none have names

but everyone knows

It burns
today it is
the will I
forget
you can
turn on the root
swallow
be seen
it bursts
be glad

Come bird
come thrush
come voices
in the woods
come
bird
bird

Is it you
my heart
that I do not believe
I want to take away
my hands

Not a single time
the word is
mentioned can it
be mentioned it is
turnable

Sound mountain
eyes
they are heard
together
destroyed
destroy hear

Now you will
be able to see
again
wave it off
after Köln
I was very afraid
and now
I can simply
not find
any word

Snow lard
phosphorus
all the time
I am
wrong

Out of the earth
forest forest
mountain
river
someone has time

The river is brown
today it
runs it
is blue
today
blue between
today it is
glad

Also they
are them
to each other

Tears they
straighten up
with which
hands
what day
I want to get to
buy
a dress
for your features
they straighten
up

Not here
I hear it
no one hears it
the sound for
darkness
can be so
many words
open the window
are you made
of words

The smoke goes into the whisp
the whisp in the smoke
do walk on your head
if you want
part human
not man

Not even they
are moving
in the forest
can we listen

Once again
I make a mistake I stand
on my toes I reach
out my hands
I am not
received

But where is
it the
light
lash snow
awe

Shift tone
love and
be silent

The river is wild
today
today
it has tears
it is poisonous
all sounds that hit
the mountain
the sun

Try then
to answer me
for real

But to

yourself

you do that

human

as one

from the word

melts

someone else

The flower is
the flower
about this
the river is
the river

I will
listen
to you
but
help me
you too
by
listening
to me

To me
you say
to me
no one has
said you

We don't really know
you know
don't we know
is it the friend
someone has time

Spring I am
anxious
many red treetops
but what is it
it is young shots

I cannot

see

the words

you

start out

from

Go numb
lard
I have to
change
my life

The sun
the forest
it is shifting
away from
us

It is
at home
where
the river
is glad

Wrote then that the water
that hears you speak
is like before
and do speak
even with the eyes
but can you
really see me

The river goes up
it lies down
just a little bit
the sun rises
I have no one
to talk to

Sounds about sounds meld

can we listen

suffer

hear a love

a love cools

it is the river

The words are names
the words are the root of
all names
as if stealing
names are nothing

You know
it is poisonous
it is open
minded
it has time

Speak
something
I beg
you speak
you too

TRANSLATOR'S NOTE

Whenever I tell anyone that I'm translating the poetry of Ann Jäderlund, they inevitably ask, "isn't that impossible?" This comes no doubt in part from the idea that poetry is untranslatable. But perhaps in the case of Jäderlund, this feeling is enhanced by the sense that her poetry is extra poetic, and thus extra untranslatable. After all, it is a poetry of heightened emotion and volatility, paired with an incredible precision.

However, the words and sentences in Jäderlund's *Lonespeech* are very simple: sun, dies, fly, voice, burns, speak. These are very translatable words! Jäderlund pushes back against this simplicity by twisting the syntax, linebreaks, enjambments. The effect is, to use a word from the book itself, "clearabout": put another way, the language she uses is "clear" but it's also "about." It doesn't arrive in a straight line. It warps.

It burns
today can
you answer

       I cannot

       hear

       speak

Through these precise, small turns of syntax and
lineation, seemingly simple, even prosaic statements
are charged with force, emotion: Jäderlund's signature.
Whether they are short fragments or longer poems with
lines that stretch, Jäderlund's poems inevitably exhibit
what I might in a nod to painting call her "gesture,"
instantly recognizable as her "hand."

However, the fallacy that this kind of heightened
poetic state is untranslatable needs some adjustment.
Because yes, every word or phrase can be
translated—though it may take some ingenuity and
creativity—but there is something in Jäderlund's
poetry that does seem "untranslatable" in its original
essence. It reminds me of Anne Carson's discussion
of Joan of Arc in her essay "Variations on the Right to
Remain Silent." Carson argues that in their strangeness,
Joan of Arc's statements refuse to comply with her
interrogator's paradigms—what Carson equates
with "cliché"—and thereby refuses to let them "own"
her experiences. In Carson's words, Jäderlund
could be said to "catastrophize" cliché. It's not that
Jäderlund's poems are untranslatable; it's that they are
fundamentally unstable. There is no stable "original" to

begin with. We cannot "own" the words, but we can bring her catastrophizing into contact with the English language.

As part of Jäderlund's catastrophizing, language itself becomes violent:

> The voice burns
> I can see the word
> it goes through the eye
> from hearing
> it is poisonous
> with clear velocity
> speak you too

Indeed, the title of the book, *Ensamtal*, is itself a kind of catastrophizing of communication. It contains several words not just joined but overlapping: *en* (one), *ensam* (lonely), *samtal* (conversation), *sam* (prefix for togetherness) and *tal* (speech). It's poetry as speech to oneself, a loneliness distilled into conversation.

Perhaps it's relevant here, as with so many of Jäderlund's books, that the language is sampled from another source. In this case it's the correspondence between poet Paul Celan and experimental novelist Ingeborg Bachmann. Jäderlund's poetry has been intensively engaged with Celan's since the 1980s. It is both apt and ironic that the work of a poet who's supposedly untranslatable is collaged from and transformed by translations of a poet also known for his untranslatability.

Both Celan and Jäderlund have always investigated sense-making. Since the 1980s, when her work ignited the infamous "Ann Jäderlund Debates" in Swedish newspapers and journals, Jäderlund has been associated with elusiveness. At that point, critics accused her of an unethical obscurantism. These charges always struck me as odd because when I read her work, I feel struck by a velocity that comes from a kind of clarity, a "clearabout" poetry. Its voice burns, penetrates the eye, is poisonous. We cannot own Jäderlund's poems, but they are not hermetic. They penetrate, poison what's around them; create a quietly sublime experience.

ACKNOWLEDGMENTS

Thanks to the following presses that have published excerpts from this book:

Circumference Magazine
Northwest Review
World Poetry Review

Thanks to the National Endowment for the Arts for a grant to work on this book.

ANN JÄDERLUND (b. 1955) has been a leading Swedish poet since the 1980s, when her books *Streamer City, Which Once Had Been Meadow*, and *Soon Into The Summer I Will Walk Out* opened up a new direction in Swedish poetry, merging elements of the baroque and the postmodern into a mysterious yet sensual poetry. Since then she has published a number of books of poetry, most recently the complete poems, *Dikter 1985-2019*, plays and translations, including an acclaimed selection of Emily Dickinson poems (*Gång på gång är skogarna rosa*). In *Lonespeech* (*Ensamtal*, 2019), Jäderlund draws on the correspondence between Paul Celan and Ingeborg Bachmann, two poets whose work her own poetry has been in dialogue with since the 1980s, to create poems that explore a poetics of Dickinsonian slantness.

JOHANNES GÖRANSSON (b. 1973) was born in Lund, Sweden, and lives in South Bend, Indiana. He is the author of nine previous books of poetry and criticism, including *Poetry Against All*, *Summer*, and *Transgressive Circulation: Essays on Translation*, and has translated numerous poets, including Aase Berg, Ann Jäderlund, Eva Kristina Olsson, Helena Boberg, and Kim Yideum. His poems, translations, and critical writings have appeared in a wide array of journals in the US and abroad, including *Fence*, *Poetry Magazine*, *Lana Turner*, and *Spoon River Review*. He is a professor at the University of Notre Dame and the publisher of Action Books.

NIGHTBOAT BOOKS

Nightboat Books, a nonprofit organization, seeks to develop audiences for writers whose work resists convention and transcends boundaries. We publish books rich with poignancy, intelligence, and risk. Please visit nightboat.org to learn about our titles and how you can support our future publications.

The following individuals have supported the publication of this book. We thank them for their generosity and commitment to the mission of Nightboat Books:

Kazim Ali • Anonymous (8) • Mary Armantrout • Jean C. Ballantyne • Thomas Ballantyne • Bill Bruns • John Cappetta • V. Shannon Clyne • Ulla Dydo Charitable Fund • Photios Giovanis • Amanda Greenberger • Vandana Khanna • Isaac Klausner • Shari Leinwand • Anne Marie Macari • Elizabeth Madans • Martha Melvoin • Caren Motika • Elizabeth Motika • The Leslie Scalapino - O Books Fund • Robin Shanus • Thomas Shardlow • Rebecca Shea • Ira Silverberg • Benjamin Taylor • David Wall • Jerrie Whitfield & Richard Motika • Arden Wohl • Issam Zineh

This book is made possible, in part, by grants from the New York City Department of Cultural Affairs in partnership with the City Council, the New York State Council on the Arts Literature Program, and the National Endowment for the Arts.